Published by Creative Education
P.O. Box 227, Mankato, Minnesota 56002
Creative Education is an imprint of The Creative Company.

DESIGN AND PRODUCTION BY **ZENO DESIGN**

Printed in the United States of America

PHOTOGRAPHS BY Alamy (Rodolfo Arpia, Shaun
Cunningham, Dennis Frates, Simon Holdcroft, Mary Evans
Picture Library, PCL, Keith Shuttlewood, Transtock Inc.,
V1), Corbis (Bettmann, Walter Bibikow, Colin McPherson/
Colin McPherson), Getty Images (STAN HONDA/AFP. Hulton
Archive, Frank Scherschel//Time Life Pictures, Time Life
Pictures/Timepix/Time Life Pictures)

LIBRARY OF CONGRESS CATALOGING-IN-PUBLICATION DATA

Musolf, Nell.
The story of Ford / by Nell Musolf.
p. cm. — (Built for success)
Includes index
ISBN-13: 978-1-58341-604-4
1. Ford Motor Company—History—Juvenile literature.
2. Automobile industry and trade—United States—
History—Juvenile literature. I. Title.

HD9710.U54F653 2008
338.7'629220973—dc22   2007014990

9 8 7 6 5 4 3 2

BUILT FOR SUCCESS

THE STORY OF

Ford

NELL MUSOLF

A vast, colorful mural depicting factory life from the early 20th century to the present. A theater showing historic footage from the early days of the Ford Motor Company. A voyage into virtual reality with chairs that swivel 360 degrees, enabling people to feel mist from spray-painting robots, sense heat from blast furnaces, and hear the rumblings of factory machinery—all while listening to original music composed and played by the Detroit Symphony Orchestra. Such is the visitor's experience at the legendary Ford Rouge Factory in Dearborn, Michigan. Renovated in 1997, the Rouge is both a journey into the past and a glimpse of the future, telling not only the story of the Ford Motor Company but also the story of Henry Ford, the man who started it all.

CHAPTER ONE

A Better Idea

Henry Ford didn't invent the automobile, but his dream of making cars an affordable luxury that almost everyone could enjoy changed the way Americans lived, worked, and played. While growing up on a farm near Dearborn, Michigan, in the 1860s, Henry was fascinated by anything mechanical.

From an early age, he enjoyed nothing more than taking things such as coffee grinders and clocks apart and then putting them back together, and he often annoyed his five younger siblings when he disassembled their toys without permission.

Henry's mechanical ability was helpful on the family farm, but Henry soon realized that farming was not for him. The boy preferred working with machines, and as his father said, "Once Henry makes up his mind about something, he isn't likely to change it." In 1880, at age 17, Henry left his father's farm and walked for half a day until he reached the city of Detroit. There he took a job as an **apprentice** in a machine shop.

While working in the machine shop, Henry saw an **internal combustion engine** for the first time. The engine, which burned gasoline inside the engine (as opposed to the steam engine, which burned fuel externally), intrigued Henry, and he began building his own engine from plans he saw in a magazine. After living in Detroit

Henry Ford, pictured here at age 30, became a success by combining ambition with mechanical genius

for three years, Henry returned to Dearborn but eventually moved back to Detroit in 1891 after marrying a young woman named Clara Ala Bryant.

In Detroit, Henry worked as a chief engineer at the Edison Illuminating Company, an electricity utility company. His job had a flexible schedule, which gave him plenty of time to experiment with his engine. After five years of tinkering, Henry attached the completed engine to an open carriage he dubbed a Quadricycle. The Quadricycle resembled two bicycles standing next to each other; it had one seat, four wheels, and an engine in the back. One rainy night in June 1896, he took his first drive in the Quadricycle. The poor weather didn't bother Henry that night, even though the Quadricycle didn't have a top on it. Neither did the fact that the Quadricycle was too big to get out of his workshop until he broke a hole in the wall to expand the doorway. All that mattered to Henry was that he'd built a horseless carriage, or automobile, and gotten it to run.

Henry wasn't the first person to devise an automobile. A Frenchman named Nicolas-Joseph Cugnot built what was probably the first automobile in 1769. It ran on steam and went two miles (3.2 km) per hour, stopping when it ran out of steam. For the next 100 years, other inventors experimented with different kinds of fuel for engines, including electricity and kerosene. In 1876, a German named Nikolaus August Otto created a gasoline-powered engine. Nine years later, another German, Gottlieb Daimler, improved the engine and attached it to a bicycle. In 1893, Charles Duryea built a successful gasoline motorcar in the United States.

Henry quickly learned that working on engines was an expensive hobby. To raise money to buy the parts he needed, he began building racing cars, with the hope that racing would expose him to possible investors. Henry won the first race he entered, and his $1,000 prize gave him the incentive to continue racing his cars, although after that first race, he limited himself to building the cars and letting other men drive them on the racetracks.

Charles Duryea (foreground) worked with his brother and fellow inventor Frank (background) to develop a gas-powered motorcar

In 1903, 40-year-old Henry, along with 11 financial backers, founded the Ford Motor Company with $28,000. Almost immediately, the company faced a major obstacle: the Association of Licensed Automobile Manufacturers threatened to close the company down barely a month after its **incorporation** because Henry wasn't a licensed automobile manufacturer. Henry had been denied a license by the association because the group wanted to keep its membership—and outside competition—small so that profits remained high. The association was very powerful due to its control of a **patent** that had been originated by New York lawyer George B. Selden.

Selden had obtained a patent for all "road locomotives" powered by internal combustion engines. Even though he didn't manufacture engines or automobiles, Selden still collected **royalties** on them. Henry didn't think Selden deserved to be paid royalties on something he hadn't designed or built, and he refused to pay them. After a long legal battle, and after losing his original case in 1909, Henry appealed and won in 1911. The courts determined that the Ford Motor Company didn't have to pay any royalties to Selden, ruling that Selden owned the patent on **two-stroke engines** only, and the Ford Motor Company used a **four-stroke engine**. Henry had won an important victory for all car manufacturers, and his battle against Selden's patent made him a popular figure with the general public.

In the early years of the 20th century, most cars were built individually by three or four men, a manufacturing process that was slow and expensive. Henry set out to change the car-building industry by replacing this time-consuming manufacturing process with one that would enable more cars to be made more quickly. The changes he had in mind would soon transform the automobile world.

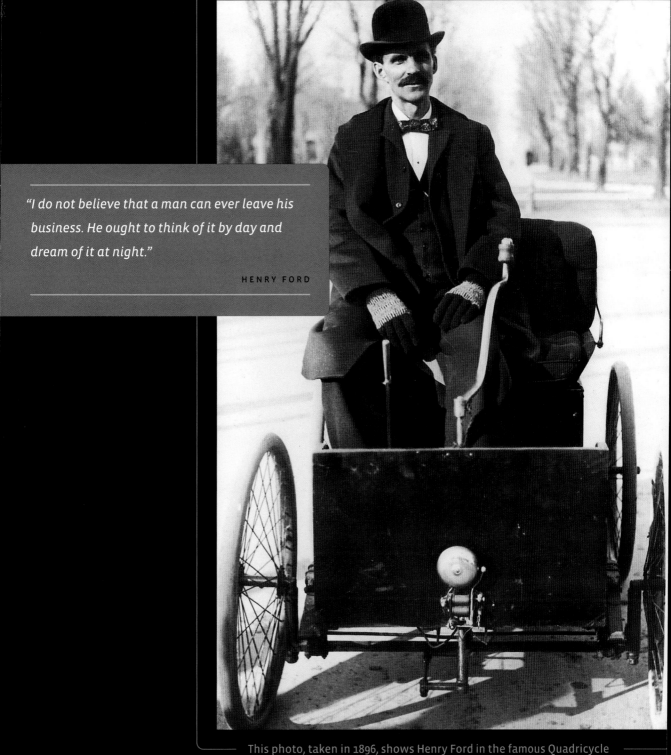

> "I do not believe that a man can ever leave his business. He ought to think of it by day and dream of it at night."
>
> HENRY FORD

This photo, taken in 1896, shows Henry Ford in the famous Quadricycle

Lucas
Capacitor discharge
ignition system
Danger high voltage

FORD

THE INTERNAL ENGINE

In an internal combustion engine like that devised by Henry Ford, a mixture of gasoline and air is burned inside a closed part called a cylinder. A piston inside the cylinder slides up and down. There are four basic engine movements: (1) The driver steps on the gas pedal, and gasoline is pumped from the fuel tank to the engine, where it mixes with air and becomes a vapor. An intake valve opens at the top of a cylinder, and the vapor is sucked in. (2) The valve closes and the piston moves upward, compressing the vapor. (3) An electric spark plug fires, lighting the vapor and causing a small explosion that pushes the piston down. (4) An outlet valve opens, and the piston moves up, pushing exhaust gases out of the cylinder. As the piston moves, it turns a crankshaft, which is linked to the driveshaft that turns the car wheels.

CHAPTER TWO

The Fords Roll By

Starting in 1903, Henry Ford used the alphabet to name his cars, starting with the Model A and then moving to Model B, Model C, and so on. When he reached the Model T in 1908, he knew he'd struck gold. "I will build a car for the great multitude," he announced. The Model T was simply designed but ruggedly built, able to handle the still mostly unpaved roads that crossed America in the early years of the 20th century.

But there was a problem with the Model T. At $825, it was still too expensive for many people to buy. Henry searched for ways to reduce production costs. He knew that if his company could make the Model T more cheaply, he could sell it at a lower price, thus enabling more people to afford this new and improved means of personal transportation—and growing the Ford brand rapidly in the process.

In 1913, after extensive research and months spent working with factory experts Frederick Winslow Taylor and Charles Sorenson, Henry concluded that the best way to build a car was to **mass-produce** it. Mass production involved taking one large task and breaking it down into several smaller tasks. Instead of having a team of men build a whole car, Henry devised a way for several men to perform

Henry Ford and his son Edsel pose here in the Model T, the most popular car of the early 1900s

one or two elements of engine building over and over again, all day long. Several other men would then assemble a different part of the car, and so on. Henry and his experts also came up with the idea of using a moving conveyor belt. Workers no longer had to get up to find a part or move to whatever they were working on; instead, the parts and the work came to them.

When Henry began producing the Model T in 1908, it took more than 12 hours to make one car. Less than 12 years later, his company would be making one car every minute. Five years after that, Ford would be producing a Model T every 10 seconds. With Model Ts being built so quickly, Henry would be able to cut the price from $780 in 1910 to a far more affordable $290 in 1925. The Model T became so popular that Henry decided it would be the only car he produced at his new automotive plant in Highland Park, Michigan.

Mass production made great business sense, but it wasn't enthusiastically received by many of the men who worked for the Ford Motor Company. Mass production built cars more quickly, but it also meant that jobs were broken down into repetitive tasks that were repeated hour after hour, day after day. Workers quit their jobs out of boredom, and **turnover** at the Ford Motor Company was high. When old workers quit, new workers needed to be trained— a time-consuming and costly cycle.

Henry wanted to keep his workers, and he knew the best way to make sure his employees were happy was to show them how much the company valued them. In a move that astonished other factory owners, Henry decided to pay his workers increased salaries. In 1914, he more than doubled the minimum wages of his workers, from $2.40 a day to $5.00 a day, an incredibly high rate of pay for that time. He also shortened the workday from nine hours to eight and the workweek from five and a half or six days to five. Lastly, he set up a profit-sharing program for his workers.

Ford's bold move was viewed as **humanitarianism** by some and madness by others. But Henry said that humanitarianism had nothing to do with it. He

Assembly-line production revolutionized manufacturing and helped the Ford brand grow at an explosive pace.

wanted to reach the largest market possible, and to do that, he needed to continue to make the Model T as cheaply as he could. Paying his workers more meant increased efficiency, which meant more cars could be built and sold, which meant more profit for Ford.

The company soon outgrew the Highland Park plant, and construction began on the Ford Rouge plant in Dearborn, Michigan, in 1917. The Rouge plant would become the largest industrial complex in the world at that time, its buildings including a tire-making facility as well as a paper mill. To supply its factories with workers, Ford sent buses into the Deep South to transport **sharecroppers** and day laborers to Michigan. There they received training to become either assembly-line workers or skilled tradesmen, such as **millwrights**, at one of the Ford plants.

While the expanding Ford brand was known primarily for its Model T, it was also building trucks and tractors. These heavy-duty counterparts to passenger vehicles were popular with farmers who needed reliable equipment. Ford introduced the Fordson tractor in 1917, during World War I. Small and inexpensive, it sold well, especially after the war ended.

Edsel Ford, Henry and Clara Ford's only child, became the president of Ford Motor Company in 1919 at the age of 26. Although Edsel lacked his father's mechanical genius, he had a strong talent for design, and he was more interested in how Ford cars looked than Henry was. In that respect, Edsel would prove to be more in touch with the evolving tastes of American consumers. "Father made the most popular car in the world," Edsel said. "I would like to make the best car in the world."

"*Every time I reduce the price of the car by one dollar, I get a thousand new customers.*"

HENRY FORD, DURING THE MODEL T'S EARLY YEARS

The Ford Company earned a following in America's heartland in part due to tractors such as the Fordson

THE ROUGE

By 1915, the Ford Motor Company had outgrown its Highland Park plant, and production began on the Rouge plant two years later. Set on a vast property along the Rouge River outside Dearborn, Michigan, the site was chosen because it could receive iron ore from Upper Michigan and coal from Pennsylvania by ship. The Rouge plant covered more than 150 acres (60 ha) and included 90 buildings, more than 90 miles (145 km) of railroad tracks, and 27 miles (44 km) of conveyer belts. The plant, which employed more than 100,000 workers, resembled a small city with its own fire station, security force, hospital, and schools. The Rouge plant had environmental policies that were ahead of their time. Ore dust from the blast furnaces was caught and melted down, and oven gases were trapped and reused as additional sources of power. When completed in 1927, the Rouge was the largest industrial complex in the world.

CHAPTER THREE

The Best Never Rest

I n the 1920s, Edsel fought hard to keep Ford
Motor Company ahead of the competition. Ford's
chief rival was the General Motors Corporation
(GMC). GMC had spent a great deal of time making
its cars—such as the Chevrolet Coupe and the plush
Cadillac—modern and appealing to the public. It
also put a lot of effort into **marketing**, largely through
print advertisements in magazines and newspapers.

In 1922, Edsel convinced Henry to buy the Lincoln Motor Company, a luxury car
maker, primarily to compete with GMC's Cadillac. Edsel had made a start in mod-
ernizing Ford, but, due to his father's stubbornly conservative ways, the process
would be a struggle for the remainder of Edsel's life.

In 1922, Ford executives joined Edsel in urging Henry to change the Model T into
something up-to-date that would attract new customers. They wanted Henry to
produce a car with more features, such as an automatic gearshift instead of the
Model T's stick shift, **hydraulic brakes** instead of **mechanical brakes**, and a choice
of color beyond the standard Ford black. Henry refused, seeing no reason to change
a car that, to him, was perfect. Edsel tried to change his father's mind, but he,

The Cadillac V-8 seven-passenger Sedan, shown here, is priced at $2945, f.o.b. Detroit. Body by Fisher. Special equipment extra. G. M. A. C. terms available on any body type.

It has been a great privilege during recent months to bring the enjoyment and the advantages of Cadillac ownership to many men and women who have long desired them, but who, for price consideration alone, have been impelled to forego them. Now, a large number of these people are driving the car of their choice—for today's Cadillac V-8, the finest eight ever produced by this organization, is also the lowest-priced Cadillac offered in many years. If you are among those who have cherished an ambition to own one of these distinguished cars, this is the time to consult the Cadillac-La Salle dealer in your community. It is quite possible that you will now find a Cadillac well within your means.

CADILLAC V 8 12 16

The elegant Cadillac was one of few cars of the early 1900s to inspire envy at the Ford Company

too, failed. Ford introduced its first pickup truck in 1925. Named the Ford Model
T Runabout, it sold well and began to build a base of customers who would remain loyal to the line. Still, in 1926, Ford sales fell from $1.87 million the year
before to $1.67 million. Faced with the losses, Henry reluctantly set to work
building a new car.

As the Ford Motor Company expanded, so did the need for supplies required
to make its cars. By 1927, Henry had implemented another time- and money-
saving strategy. Instead of buying automobile parts from other manufacturers
and then putting his cars together, Henry wanted to have control over everything that went into Ford automobiles. So he bought iron and coal mines, for-
ests, mills, and additional factories where workers could get the materials they
needed when they needed them.

A second Model A was introduced in 1928 and was an instant hit with the
public; dealers placed 727,000 orders for the new vehicle before it was even on
the market. Once Henry had introduced the new Model A, however, he again
refused to do any more updating on it.

In spite of the company's expansion and popularity, times were tough at Ford,
as they were throughout the rest of America, during the 1930s. A **depression** had
hit the economy, and thousands of Americans were out of work. Money for new
cars was scarce, and there were other problems at Ford as well. **Labor unions**
were growing stronger. The unions wanted to organize automobile industry
workers so that the workers would have more control over their salaries and
benefits. Believing his workers were already treated fairly, Henry resented the
labor unions' attempts to interfere with the way he ran his company.

In 1935, the National Labor Relations Board ruled that the Ford Motor
Company had violated the Wagner Act, which stated that workers had the right
to bargain as a group for fair wages and better treatment. The situation got
worse in 1937, when union organizers who were passing out workers' rights fly-
ers at the Rouge plant were attacked by men who worked for Henry. Reporters

The second generation of Ford's Model A assumed several different styles or forms, including that of a van

published photographs of the attack and the fight that followed it. Workers went on **strike**, leaving Ford no choice but to **negotiate** a labor contract.

"We must be the great arsenal of democracy," said President Franklin D. Roosevelt when he banned civilian car production in 1941 immediately following Japan's surprise attack on the U.S. naval base at Pearl Harbor, Hawaii. Roosevelt wanted all car manufacturers to focus on building military equipment, and Ford assembly plants stopped building cars and instead produced tanks and tank parts, aircraft engines, and army jeeps. The production would continue until World War II's end in 1945, at which time Ford's plants resumed building cars, trucks, and farm equipment.

In 1943, Edsel Ford died of cancer at the age of 49. With Edsel gone, Clara Ford and Edsel's widow, Eleanor, banded together to ensure that Edsel's son, Henry II, would take over the company. Convinced that the time had come for 80-year-old Henry to retire, they told the auto baron that they would sell their company **stock** if he didn't step down and allow Henry II to take control. Eventually, Henry agreed. In 1945, 28-year-old Henry Ford II became president of the Ford Company. At that time, the company was losing an estimated $10 million every month due to the war's effects on manufacturing and consumer spending. Economic conditions after the war would be slow to improve. Henry Ford's grandson clearly had his work cut out for him.

On April 7, 1947, Henry Ford died at Fair Lane, his 56-room mansion in Dearborn, Michigan. During the course of his long life, Henry had enjoyed a truly spectacular career. At the time of his death, his personal fortune was worth $500 million, and he had sold 15,456,868 Model Ts. His single-minded vision of making an affordable car for the average consumer had changed American transportation forever.

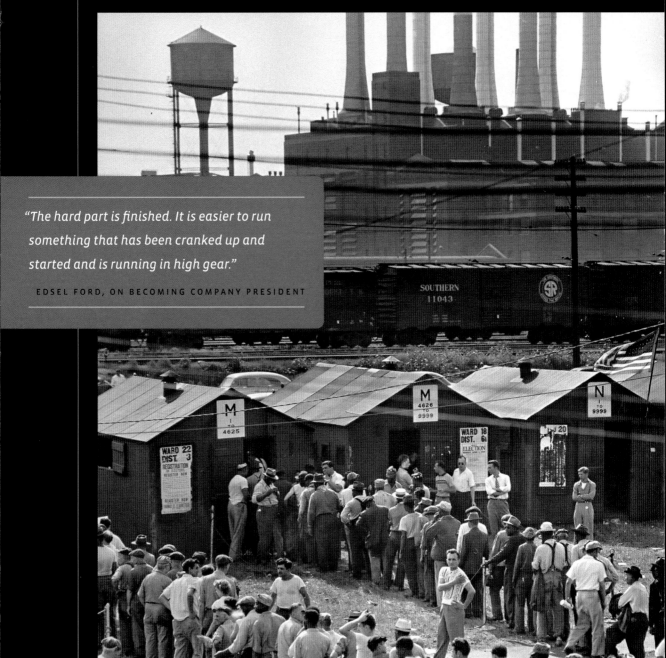

Ford was plagued by labor disputes in the 1930s and '40s; pictured are Ford workers voting to strike

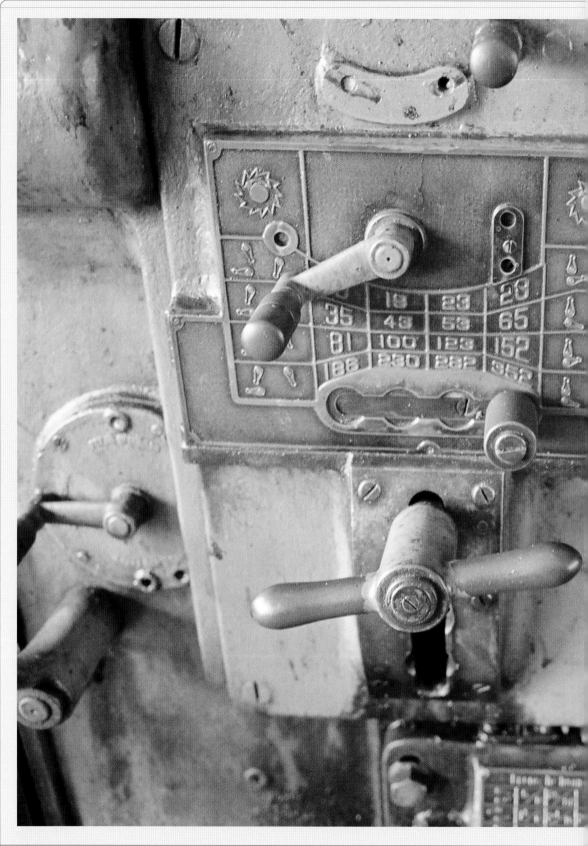

Abandoned machinery from Fordlandia

FORDLANDIA

Not all of Henry Ford's plans to control everything that went into the production of his cars was a success. In 1929, Henry began work on Fordlandia, a rubber plantation in the Amazon rainforests of Brazil. There he planned to grow rubber trees that would eventually become rubber tires for his automobiles. An entire village resembling a typical American suburb was created, complete with a paved main street, running water in the homes of executives, and a shopping center with tailors, restaurants, and shoemakers for the workers at the rubber plant. Initially, Fordlandia attracted many local workers. Ford paid 37 cents a day for field hands, which was approximately double the going rate in the area. But due to labor problems, crop blight, and generally poor planning, Fordlandia never became the tire-producing factory that Henry had envisioned, and it closed in 1945 after an economical synthetic rubber was developed.

CHAPTER FOUR

Quality Is Job One

After World War II, Americans were eager to put the hardships and sacrifices of the war behind them and to have fun again. For many people, part of enjoying themselves included owning a car that was not only safe and reliable, but a pleasure to drive and look at as well. Like his father Edsel, Henry Ford II recognized that consumers wanted cars that were well-made, attractive, and comfortable.

To assist him in building such products, Henry II hired a group of 10 young U.S. Air Force statistical experts, who became known as the "Whiz Kids," to reconstruct the company's financial management system.

Ford introduced the Thunderbird and the Fairlane to the American public in 1955. Marketed as "personal luxury cars," the Thunderbird and Fairlane were about as far from a Model T as could be imagined. The Thunderbird's small size and powerful engine attracted buyers looking for a sporty, thrilling ride. When first unveiled, the Thunderbird was a two-seater that combined a clean, linear appearance with comfort and speed. The Thunderbird would undergo many cosmetic changes but remain a constant presence in Ford's lineup until 1997.

The Thunderbird represented a flashy new direction for Ford—especially when it was painted red

The Fairlane began as a big vehicle intended to accommodate growing families. It would fluctuate in size over the next 10 years, shrinking to a midsize car in the early '60s before growing slightly larger again in the mid-1960s. In 1968, Ford would begin phasing out the name "Fairlane" and would eventually replace it with the new name "Torino."

Another Ford car introduced in the 1950s was the Edsel. Named in honor of Edsel Ford and unveiled in 1958, the highly stylized, heavily grilled car was designed to be distinctly recognizable from any perspective. Unfortunately, no one seemed to like the way the Edsel looked from any direction. Marketing surveys later found that in addition to disliking the Edsel's appearance, people also disliked the name "Edsel." It sounded old-fashioned and was one of several reasons the Edsel failed to appeal to buyers. While the Edsel would later become a sought-after collectible, at the time it was introduced, it was a colossal failure. Only 84,000 Edsels were produced, and in 1959, after Ford presented the 1960 model, the line was discontinued.

On January 17, 1956, the public was allowed, for the first time, to buy stock in the Ford Motor Company. By the end of that day, 10.2 million **shares** of stock had been sold, giving Ford approximately 350,000 new **stockholders**. People outside of the Ford family now owned 22 percent of the business, and the Ford Motor Company went from a private company to a publicly owned one, earning $650 million in the process.

Ford continued to unveil new car designs in the 1960s. In 1964, both the Mustang and the GT40 were introduced. The Mustang, with its muscular appearance and low price tag, was a huge and immediate hit with young people. "We believe the Mustang represents a new dimension in American motoring," said Ford Motor Company vice president Lee Iacocca in 1964. "It offers a combination of driving fun, roominess, and style ... all at a low initial cost." The GT40 was the result of Henry II's desire to have a Ford in the famous Le Mans automobile race held annually in France. The car represented the company well, as

With its massive grill and bulging headlights, the Edsel was one of the most distinctive Fords ever built.

a Ford GT40 won the Le Mans four straight times, from 1966 to 1969.

By the 1970s, people were becoming more aware of the need to care for the environment, and Ford joined other car makers in producing small or compact vehicles that consumed less fuel and thus produced less pollution. Released in 1971, the Pinto was a fashionable Ford compact that seemed ideal for the cost- and fuel-conscious times. Unfortunately, when involved in rear-end collisions, several Pintos suffered fuel tank explosions, resulting in severe accidents and many lawsuits from the people involved.

Ford received a great deal of negative publicity over the accident-prone Pinto. Critics alleged that Ford was aware of the design flaws in the Pinto's gas tank but purposely chose not to correct them in an effort to save money, a charge that Ford denied. In 1978, Ford was forced to **recall** all affected Pintos. The company lost millions of dollars and gained the unfortunate reputation of being a corporation that put profits ahead of safety. Ford would stop production on the Pinto entirely in 1981 and begin the slow process of repairing its damaged image.

The late 1970s saw another major change at Ford. In 1979, after 34 years of running the family company, Henry II decided to retire. At that time, the Ford Motor Company was the fourth-largest corporation in the world, making $43 billion a year. Henry II's successor, Philip Caldwell, an employee of Ford since 1953, became the first person outside the Ford family to head the company. Caldwell had previously headed Ford's truck operations, the Philco computer division, and its international operations. By focusing on manufacturing quality, research, and employee satisfaction, the new president hoped to help Ford recover its reputation following the Pinto disaster.

> *"I bought a pretty cool wagon and we call it a Woodie...."*
>
> *SURF CITY* SONG LYRICS, BY JAN AND DEAN

As president, Henry Ford II (right) unveiled such popular models as the Thunderbird and Mustang

THE "WOODIE" WAGON

One of the most peculiar cars of the 1940s was the Ford Super Deluxe Wagon. Introduced in 1940 and sometimes called "furniture on wheels," the Super Deluxe used real wood as side paneling and on the instrument panel. The so-called "Woodie" became especially popular among surfers in the 1960s. Successful bands of the time, such as the Beach Boys and Jan and Dean, mentioned the Woodie in several of their songs. Surfers were even known to cut up the wood on their Woodies when they needed emergency surfboards. A great deal of wood was needed to make a Ford Super Deluxe, and by 1949, the car had become too expensive to manufacture. Later, "wood" trims on cars weren't really wood at all; wood-grained decals and plastic appliqués were used instead. Time, rain, and snow were hard on Woodies, and a completely restored Woodie is one of the rarest of collectible vehicles today.

CHAPTER FIVE

The Road Ahead

Early in Caldwell's reign as president, Ford introduced one of its most popular vehicles ever: the Taurus. When the Taurus came out in 1985, its futuristic looks caused some people to describe it as a "jelly bean" or a "flying potato." The vehicle's smooth lines were a big change from the boxy "gas-guzzlers" that had preceded it.

A midsize car with front-wheel drive, the Taurus handled well and was fuel-efficient, making it popular from the moment it was introduced. In 1986, its first full year on the market, more than 263,000 were sold. In 1992, the Taurus would be the best-selling car in America, with sales close to 410,000, and it would remain the top seller for five years in a row—a longer run as the industry leader than even the famous Model T. Except for a brief hiatus in 2006, the Taurus would remain in production year after year, incurring several design changes along the way.

The 1990s saw the Ford Motor Company's offerings continue to expand. In 1990, the Ford Aerostar minivan was named *Motor Trend*'s Truck of the Year, and the Lincoln Town Car was named Car of the Year. And in 1991, the Ford Explorer was introduced. A mid-sized sport utility vehicle (SUV), the Explorer quickly became a best seller and was credited with making the SUV one of the most popular types of vehicle on the road. While the Explorer and Aerostar rose in popularity, the

time, the fashionable Explorer was involved. The **tire tread** on some Explorers separated from the tire. This caused the tire to disintegrate and, often, the vehicle to veer off the road and roll over. Many serious injuries and several deaths were attributed to such rollovers. As a result, both Ford and Firestone, the manufacturer of the Explorer's tires, faced a storm of criticism. Eventually, Firestone was found to be responsible, a product recall was announced in 2001, and Explorer owners were able to exchange their faulty tires for new ones.

In 2003, Bill Ford, Henry Ford's great-grandson, was named executive chairman of the Ford Motor Company. A lifelong nature enthusiast, Bill sought to strengthen Ford's environmental standards and increase development in its hybrid division. Hybrid vehicles, first unveiled in 1997, drove cleaner and more quietly than traditional cars by using two or more power sources—gasoline plus electric batteries, for example. The Ford Escape, a small SUV hybrid introduced in 2004, was capable of traveling up to 500 miles (805 km) on one tank of fuel, or approximately 40 percent farther than the non-hybrid Escape. "Our customers are increasingly concerned about the price of gasoline, air quality, oil supply issues, and the effects of CO_2 emissions on climate change," said Bill Ford. "At the same time, they tell us how much they appreciate the versatility and capability of our SUVs. They don't want to give them up, and we don't think they should have to."

Ford's F-Series truck line, which had maintained a strong following since 1948, remained robust in the new millennium. The F-Series of pickup trucks set a new sales record for the automobile industry in July 2005, selling 126,905 trucks over the course of the month. "Over the past 57 years, no vehicle has been more

The Ford Escape hybrid combined the SUV style that many Americans preferred with better fuel economy

"and it just keeps getting stronger."

In 2006, Bill Ford decided to step down as Ford's executive chairman. After stating that he at times felt overwhelmed by the job of running the company his great-grandfather had started, Ford appointed Alan Mulally as his successor. Mulally was a former vice president of Boeing, a company that manufactures airplanes, and Ford had been impressed by the way Mulally had successfully run Boeing's commercial airplane division in the late 1990s.

In 2007, Ford announced a collaboration with the computer software giant Microsoft Corporation to bring Microsoft's Sync technology to Ford vehicles. Sync, a voice-activated connection between personal electronic devices—such as phones and portable music players—and cars, was to be available in all Ford cars and trucks by 2009. Sync was designed to improve road safety by letting drivers make phone calls or select music while keeping both hands on the steering wheel. After an initial setup, users would be able to download future versions and upgrades of the system via a Web site or at a Ford dealership.

The Ford Motor Company started out more than a century ago as one man's vision to build a horseless carriage that could be bought and enjoyed by the average working person. It went far beyond that first dream, touching millions of lives in ways that Henry Ford probably never imagined. A 2004 advertising campaign described Fords as "built for the road ahead." No matter how smooth or rough that road might be, Ford is sure to be there.

"We want to have an even bigger impact in our next 100 years than we did in our first 100."

BILL FORD, FORD EXECUTIVE CHAIRMAN

Microsoft's Sync voice-controlled technology promised to increase convenience and safety in future vehicles

FORD INTERNATIONAL

Ford is often thought of as an "all-American" company due to its deep Michigan roots and the huge success it has enjoyed in the United States. But Henry Ford's company has had a presence in countries far from American shores since as early as the 1920s. One of Ford's best foreign markets has long been the United Kingdom, the source of two of Ford's international vehicle brands: Jaguar and Land Rover. Ford also owns the Volvo brand of Sweden and has manufacturing plants in many countries, including Canada, Mexico, Brazil, Germany, Australia, and China. The company has a smaller presence in Asia but does have partial ownership in the Mazda company of Japan. Certain Ford models are often made specifically for certain countries, but some models have proven to have great international appeal. The Ford Focus, for instance, has sold well on two continents since it was unveiled in Europe in 1998 and North America in 2000.

GLOSSARY

apprentice a person learning a craft under a skilled worker

depression a period of financial and industrial decline; the Great Depression of the 20th century started in 1929 and lasted throughout the 1930s

four-stroke engine an internal combustion engine that operates using four piston strokes per every two rotations of an engine's crankshaft; it is the most commonly used engine for automotive and industrial purposes

humanitarianism a belief that it is a person's duty to look out for the well-being of other people

hydraulic brakes a system for braking, or stopping a moving vehicle, in which force is applied to a pedal and is transferred to the brake pad via oil under pressure

incorporation the act of forming a firm or company into a corporation by completing all of the required procedures and paperwork

internal combustion engine an engine in which the process of combustion (the burning of fuel) takes place inside one or more cylinders

labor unions organizations of employees that negotiate salaries and other benefits with their employers

marketing advertising and promoting a product in order to increase sales

mass-produce to make large quantities of a product, usually by machine

mechanical brakes a system for braking, or stopping a moving vehicle, in which force is applied to a pedal or handle and is transferred via simple mechanical connections to the brake pad

millwrights people who design, build, or repair factory machinery

negotiate to confer with others in order to reach a compromise or agreement

patent an official document that says who has the right to use, make, or sell an invention

recall to call back, or ask customers to return, all copies of a product that might be defective

royalties shares, or a percentage, of a product's proceeds paid to someone in exchange for an endorsement or other valuable contribution

sharecroppers people who farm land for someone else and are paid a share of whatever is grown

shares the equal parts a company may be divided into; shareholders each own a certain number of shares, or a percentage, of the company

stock shared ownership in a company by many people who buy shares, or portions, of stock, hoping the company will make a profit and the stock value will increase

stockholders people or corporations who own shares of stock (portions of ownership) in a corporation

strike a protest, usually over low wages or poor working conditions, that involves the refusal to do work

tire tread the thick outer surface of a tire; the portion that touches the road

turnover the number of workers replaced in a business or industry in a specified period

two-stroke engines internal combustion engines that operate using two piston strokes per every two rotations of an engine's crankshaft; they are most commonly found in small, lightweight machines such as lawn mowers and scooters

SELECTED BIBLIOGRAPHY

Adler, Dennis. *The Art of the Automobile*. New York: HarperCollins, 2000.

Blue Oval News. "Homepage." http://www.blueovalnews.com.

The Ford Motor Company. "Homepage." http://www.ford.com.

The Henry Ford Museum and Greenfield Village. "Homepage." The Henry Ford. http://www.hfmgv.org.

Lasky, Victor. *Never Complain, Never Explain*. New York: Richard Marek Publishers, 1981.

Neyhart, Louise. *Henry Ford, Engineer*. Boston: Houghton Mifflin, 1950.

INDEX

D0688107

Eat Your Colors

Red
Food
Fun

by Lisa Bullard

Mankato, Minnesota

A+ Books are published by Capstone Press,
151 Good Counsel Drive, P.O. Box 669, Mankato, Minnesota 56002.
www.capstonepress.com

1 2 3 4 5 6 11 10 09 08 07 06

Library of Congress Cataloging-in-Publication Data
Bullard, Lisa.
Red food fun / Lisa Bullard.
    p. cm.— (A+ books. Eat your colors)
    Includes bibliographical references and index.
    ISBN-13: 978-0-7368-5383-5 (hardcover)
    ISBN-10: 0-7368-5383-9 (hardcover)
    1. Food—Juvenile literature. 2. Red—Juvenile literature. I. Title. II. Series.
TX355.B9285 2006
641.3–dc22   2005025835

Summary: Brief text and colorful photos describe common foods that are the color red.

Credits
Erika L. Shores, editor; Kia Adams, designer; Kelly Garvin, photo researcher

Photo Credits
Capstone Press/Karon Dubke, all

Note to Parents, Teachers, and Librarians
This Eat Your Colors book uses full-color photographs and a nonfiction format to introduce children to the color red. *Red Food Fun* is designed to be read aloud to a pre-reader or to be read independently by an early reader. Photographs help listeners and early readers understand the text and concepts discussed. The book encourages further learning by including the following sections: Recipe, Glossary, Read More, Internet Sites, and Index. Early readers may need assistance using these features.

Table of Contents

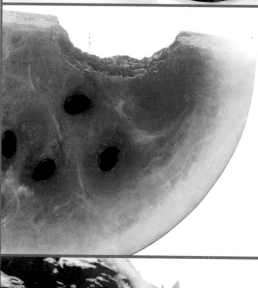

Red Food Fun

Fruity, juicy, sticky, and spicy. Red foods make super snacks. What is your favorite red food?

Delicious red apples
float in a tub. Bobbing
for apples is a fun
party game.

Plump red cherries fill
a pie. Cherry trees bloom
with pink blossoms before
the cherries begin to grow.

Spicy Red Foods

Red spaghetti sauce oozes over squiggly noodles. The sauce gets its red color from smashed tomatoes.

Pepperoni is a peppy
kind of red sausage.
Round pepperoni slices
add spice to your pizza.

Salsa is the Spanish word for sauce. Juicy red tomatoes and hot, spicy peppers give salsa its kick.

Juicy Red Foods

The hollow part of a red
raspberry helps you
hold it on your finger.
Eat them one by one
for a tart treat.

Cranberry juice is
full of tangy flavor.
It takes about 275 tiny
red cranberries to
make one glass of juice.

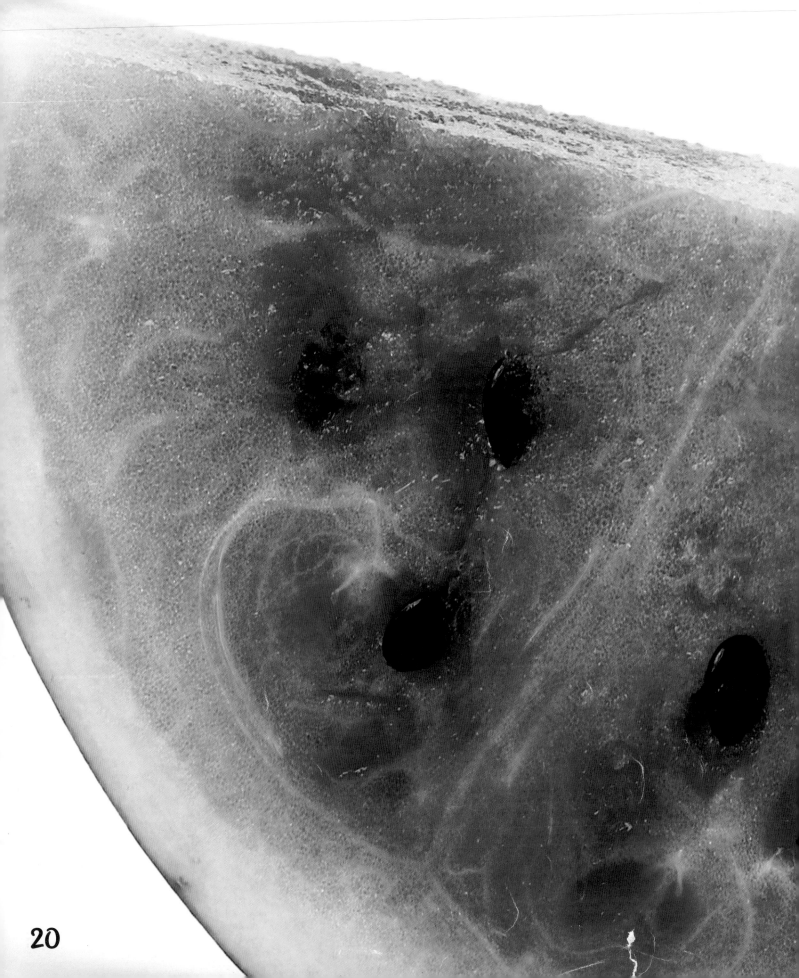

Don't let the green outside fool you. The watermelon's insides are rosy red.

Cherry tomatoes look like red polka dots in a green salad. Each little tomato bursts with juicy flavor.

Sticky Red Foods

Sticky red strawberry jam is a sweet treat. Jam is jelly with chunks of fruit.

A squiggly line of red ketchup tastes great on a hot dog. Aren't red foods lots of fun?

Happy Pizza Face

You can make your very own pizza face for a yummy after-school snack.

What You Will Need

1 pre-sliced English muffin

Pizza sauce

Grated mozzarella cheese

Pepperoni slices

Green olives

Toaster oven or microwave

How to Make a Happy Pizza Face

1. Open the English muffin.

2. Top one half with a thin layer of pizza sauce.

3. Next, place grated mozzarella cheese over the sauce.

4. Then put two pepperoni slices on your pizza. Ask an adult to cut a green olive in slices. Put them on top of the pepperoni slices for eyes. Have an adult cut another pepperoni slice into a smile.

5. An adult should help you with the toaster oven or microwave. Bake your pizza until the cheese is melted.

6. Carefully remove your pizza from the toaster oven or microwave. Wait a few minutes for your pizza face to cool. Eat and enjoy! Start over and make the other half into another happy pizza face!

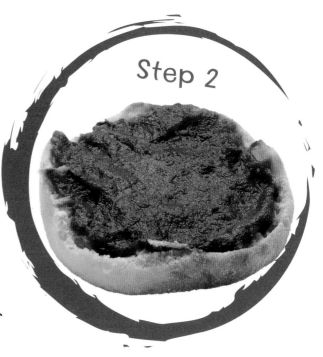

Step 2

Step 3

Step 4

Glossary

jam (JAM)—a sweet, thick food made from boiled fruit and sugar

salsa (SAHL-suh)—a hot, spicy tomato sauce that can be flavored with onions and hot peppers

sausage (SAW-sij)—chopped and seasoned meat stuffed into a thin case shaped like a tube; most pepperoni comes sliced into circles.

tart (TART)—a sour or sharp taste

Read More

Schuette, Sarah L. *Red*. Colors. Mankato, Minn.: Capstone Press, 2003.

Whitehouse, Patricia. *Red Foods*. The Colors We Eat. Chicago: Heinemann, 2002.

Internet Sites

FactHound offers a safe, fun way to find Internet sites related to this book. All of the sites on FactHound have been researched by our staff.

Here's how:

1. Visit *www.facthound.com*

2. Type in this special code **0736853839** for age-appropriate sites. Or enter a search word related to this book for a more general search.

3. Click on the Fetch It button.

FactHound will fetch the best sites for you!

Index